BEDTIME STORIES FOR A LADY OF A CERTAIN AGE

LLOYDA ALBACH

First Edition

PAGE PUBLISHING, INC.
New York, NY

First originally published by Page Publishing, Inc. 2018

ISBN 978-1-64138-811-5 (Paperback)
ISBN 978-1-64138-814-6 (Digital)

Printed in the United States of America

Dedicated to The Two-Legged and
Four-Legged Loves of My Life

Contents

INTERMISSION

(No pretty Music Will Play)

BUT

YOU MAY READ

The Favorites

A sweet glimpse into the Seasons,

which composes a lifetime

Read on…Ladies!

TRANSITIONING

From

Fun With The Favorites

To MAGIC

....Next Page, Please!

The Prologue for A Lady of a Certain Age My Contact Sport

For me, writing is a contact sport! Pencil in hand, mood music playing, it's all systems go! Words flow onto the paper as I eye my most important piece of equipment, a very soft rubber eraser! It's basic time, trial and error. Later will follow a journey into the world of digital print, editors, and publishers. Success will follow!

In the beginning it's jog the imagination, dream a little, and troll for words. My buddy is Webster's Dictionary. Words, words, words!

I love them as they evoke my eighty-two-year-old imagination.

Some days I am a mad scientist, riveted to a whimsical Frankenstein's monster. Other days my task of writing is ethereal. Words flutter and float like a wood sprite with words aligning in just the right order to form my vignette. Words just flow, and they paint a picture for me. The process if just plain fun!

For this Lady of a Certain Age, writing is a contact sport. It keeps my mind vital and in gear. Mental workouts stave off senior moments and keep me on the track for staying independent.

Writing is a win-win situation for me, and I hope you enjoy my literary endeavors. I invite you to adventure into my Bedtime Stories. May you laugh a lot, and maybe shed a tear or two. As you know our time is precious! *Rock on, ladies!*

Jack

The first time I saw Jack Albach, I was walking down the senior stairs at Kemper Hall to meet my blind date for the Freshman Tea Dance. As I came down the stairs, there he stood, next to Mrs. Birmingham, to be properly introduced to me.

As I came to the foot of the stairs, I was awestruck by this handsome, St. John's Cadet. Jack was tall and blonde, with the most beautiful, laughing, blue eyes with a cleft in his chin. My heart melted when he took my hand (which incidentally wasn't clammy). He then walked me across the campus to Nash House for the Freshman Tea Dance.

Jack was sixteen and I was fourteen, and we were *oh* so grown up! The dance was between four to six in the afternoon and very well chaperoned. The year was 1949.

Thus began a lifetime of adventures and misadventures with my one true love.

The Mother Superior of my convent school, Kemper Hall, happened to be standing behind what turned out to be our "kissing tree." *Whoops!* The Mother was not pleased with my decorum!

After the dance was over and Jack's St. John's bus had left, I told my roommate, Sherry, "I wish to marry Jack Albach someday." Six years later, my wish came true!

Of course, Jack and I had our share of heartaches, but growing up in the Midwest, we had similar values and were always there to support each other.

During the tragic times, Jack knew the right things to say to make me smile and soothe my soul. He was "The Wind Beneath My Wings."

Always I was there for Jack, too. We complimented each other. He was the kind, easy-going, gentle soul, while I have always been the stubborn overthinker with a tendency to explode to get things done.

My most infamous meltdown was hitting Jack over the head with a homemade pizza, straight out of the oven. Jack took a very dim view of this, but could you blame him? In the family, this escapade is known as "Mom's Pizza Party." (Yes, too many martinis were involved).

It was not always "Moon-Spoon + June." What marriage is? But we had a lifetime of love and respect for each other, which is eternal.

Our lives were a wild adventure chasing jet planes around the world. We had three precious children and an assortment of loveable pets, including horney toads and a half-dead mongrel dog we nursed back to health. He was a castaway Christmas pup, overgrown with a too-tight red ribbon tied around his neck. It was instant love for our son, John. We took this bedraggled pup to our vet, who proclaimed, "We have to put this dog down!" John bargained to take the mangy creature home for the weekend to try a little love, kindness, and good food. John was smitten and called his mangy love Herald, and by Monday, Herald was better. He was all John's...a loopy tongue, no tooth miracle! Herald lived to be nineteen!

Love is a powerful medicine! Jack and I truly loved each other and our family, even Herald!

After fifty-eight years of marriage, Jack died gently here in our home one sunny Sunday afternoon. We had the best life has to give, and Jack's essence has never left me.

From the time I met Jack, he was "Drop-Dead-Gorgeous," but the last thing I expected was for the mortician's first words to be, Mrs. Albach, "You have such a handsome husband, and he has had such great care." This made me smile as Jack never would have expected a compliment after death.

There were piles of papers to sign, but this genuine gentleman told me to call him in the morning and we could do the paperwork. Then with great dignity, he took Jack from our home for the last time.

The next morning I called Direct Funeral Services Crematory only to hear, "This number has been disconnected?" What a shock! Whom did I give my husband and our children's father to? Next I called Hospice only to have them take three hours to find out the telephone lines were down on the other side of town.

Jack was never lost, and yes, God does have a sense of humor!

Beauty

Kim Sherrill Albach, our first-born, entered this world a beautiful, baby girl. Jack and I were awed by Kim, not only by her beauty, but also by her sunny nature.

When Kim was a newborn the maternity ward nurses used her for bath demonstration. Kim was a flawless eight pound, “Rosey Bambino” with a cute brown curl and dancing eyes.

At sixty, Kim is still my “Rosey Bambino.” She is a Nurse Practioner, Zumba Instructor and also a National Champion Fat Tire Bike racer. She is TOP in her age group today!

Kim is an athletic beauty whose goodness emulates from her being. She is the perfect wife for her husband Jan Bear. To know Kim is to love and admire her.

In the dictionary the name Kim Bear should be the definition for FAITHFUL and FRIEND. I love my precious daughter, Kim.... A MILLION SUGARS!!

P.S.—I Love You

In many families there is a baby who is an afterthought. In fact our Shawn wasn't even an afterthought!

This bouncing baby boy miraculously arrived after a fabulous and fun Officer's Wives Club Charity Ball??? On December 27, 1963 Shawn Michael Albach arrived the spitting image of his father Jack, hairy arms and all! Being six years younger than his siblings, and not having a spare bedroom in our captain's quarters, Jack and I decided to put Shawn's crib in the "L" shape area of the kitchen.

All the attention Shawn got living in the kitchen made him a smiley, happy, baby boy. He learned to talk before he could walk!

Shawn's whole life has been a Surprise! The funny baby, and then a less than Rhodes scholar in school is now my go to support system in my eighties. What a dear man Shawn is!

My Shawn knows me better than I know myself, and if I drop dead tomorrow there is nothing we have left unsaid! OH! What fun Shawn has been for both Jack and me…"P.S.—I love you!"

Traveling Through My Eighties

1. I can say or do anything and it's explained by, "You know she is in her eighties!"
2. The music in the movie theaters sounds just about right!
3. Young men make a fuss over me, which makes me feel young and gay… (HAPPY!) You're never too old to flirt your skirts!
4. Time to discover the absolute delight of shopping the treasure trove of the Dollar Store!

5. I never thought watching the trajectory of the path I walk would hold the key to my longevity!
6. When making a profound statement forgetting what I'm talking about. (Does this register, ladies)? I think this is referred to as "*brain fog!*"
7. Being asked to tell a famous, family story and I have no memory it ever happened.
8. Keep doing! "Evil succeeds when the good stand by and do nothing!"
9. Take mañana out of your vocabulary! It may never arrive!
10. To end, My Funniest What Ever!

Earl, a very elderly friend, called me and asked, "Who the Hell are you? You're on my Christmas card list, and I can't remember who you are." Sometimes, I can't remember "Who I "are" either!"

Slipping South

When I write about slipping south, it's not about crossing the Mason-Dixon Line. It's about my skin slipping south in a surprising number of areas!

First my face... *Who* is that looking back at me from the mirror? (I saw a picture of Willie Nelson on the front of the *Inquirer*, and I noticed a resemblance)! I am beginning to think smile lines are cool for this Lady of a Certain Age. My eyes look familiar but are not the dark, dark brown they used to be.

I have high cheekbones, but covering them are ribald, rivulets of wrinkles, streaming southward across my cheeks. These myriad wrinkles I call *crinkles* because they show character!

My nose is still my nose, but my lips refuse to keep lipstick where I put it. Lipstick W-A-N-D-E-R-S…and you know what I mean! There are times these wandering rivulets of red make me look like a vampire having just drunk blood…So much for kissable lips!

Of course I have a turkey neck! Don't all We Ladies of a Certain Age? (Scarves and turtle necks are great for camouflage)! One of my daily exercises is pivoting my neck. This is a nice trick my car insurance company is enthusiastic about!

Attached to my torso are two scrawny arms ending in multiblotched hands. (They work just fine so I'm not complaining)!

If I torque my arm at the elbow, here come those rivulets of wrinkles cascading down my arm! (So much for the glamorous, sleeveless look of my youth)!

Now for my observation of my bust line in the bathroom mirror. The perky days are long gone! No more "knockers up!" Solution! I have found "enhanced" sports bras (thank you, Mia Hamm) do wonders for my figure! I no longer have to struggle with those confounded hooks and eyes!

If you want a good laugh, try on a pair of hip-huggers in front of a full-length mirror! Better yet, try on a thong!

I was born long-waisted, but am experiencing middle-aged spread in my eighties. My torso seems to be migrating south, like a collapsing accordion. Having stood 5'7 ½" I am now 5'5". Where did I go? Nobody has thrown water on me like the wicked witch in the Wizard of Oz!

When I asked my granddaughter J. J. (the physical therapist) why I was melting, she said, "Gran, your intervertebral disks are drying out. You have twenty-three discs, one between each vertebra. When they dry out, you really do get shorter." The upside is I'm too old to get herniated discs!

To me this was very interesting although a bit technical. This may also explain why my backside is rounder, flabbier, and more fully packed than in my youth!

My legs work really well in spite of varicose veins, brown spots, mysterious purple bruises, assorted bumps, etc. (I'm not complaining, just commenting)!

Now holding up "my miracle of motion" are two size 10 feet with a toe or two splaying. My antique feet walk just fine; I no longer have more bounce to the ounce. It's steady as she goes. Remember "The Hare and the Tortoise!"

Being one lucky Lady of a Certain Age, I am still able to do everything I love. Throwing in a catnap is beneficial and writing this book keeps my old mind in gear! Yes, I'm in a measured time of life both physically and mentally, but *I am not a spent force*! Great attitudes make for wonder-filled days!

The Color Pop

Bright colors are a friend to us Ladies of a Certain Age. I found my octogenarian style, and then I made it *pop* with bright accent colors I love! If not now, when? And mañana certainly isn't in my vocabulary!

Black and white make me feel drab and dreary and don't make people sparkle when they see me.

Now, I'm "the fashionista of color," and I bring a smile to people's faces when they greet me. There is a fine line between "The clown look" and being creative with color!

I love the multicolored shoes that are so popular now. My mother always said, "Put your best foot forward, dear!"

Never do I try to emulate "the teenyboppers" but borrow those wonderful "in" colors…I don't want to look like your garden variety of grandma!

One thing I love that's very "in" is the neon-colored sports bras. They look terrific peeking out of ladylike tops. These sports bras with the racer back are a godsend. They are easy to get on and off, and no hooks or droopy straps. Wow! And they are so comfortable. Try one! You'll like it!

These wide-strapped, vivid-colored sports bras hold my shoulders back and help me stand straight…I was going to say stand tall, but tall went by the wayside with my intervertebral discs drying out (sounds like my spine is destined to be a specimen in a biology lab). I used to be 5'7 ½" and I am now 5'5".

Strangers, if they find out how old I am, say, "I want to embrace my age the way you do!" I don't think I am that fascinating, but I am refreshing, being a dilettante with color.

Regardless of my age, I plan to keep my moxie and never become obsolete. Come grow old with me and channel your inner Maven! We've earned every wrinkle so embrace this different kind of beauty with grace and dignity. A grateful heart goes a long way these days to emulate that "Joie de Vivre!"

Tickle My Funny Bone

As time goes by, we Ladies of a Certain Age have to work at keeping relevant, while putting on a happy face! Conversely, we definitely don't want to sit like a bump on a pickle and live in the land of gloom and doom!

I have read there are no grumpy centenarians, so let's get on the "Tickle My Funny Bone Train!"

Knock me over with a feather! It's amazing how much verve we can come up with when we put a little snap in our step. Just don't permit yourself to marinate in "The Miseries!"

Being a Crybaby is not allowed for us! We don't Cry Wolf, *but* if we feel something is getting off kilter with our bodies, it's time to call for help! Just go ahead and bother somebody! I did and here I am writing this book!

If you keep quiet when you think you feel "squirrelly," you may end up making a quick exit from this life and Light Beaming… somewhere?

So…It's time to pull ourselves up by our boot straps! Keep a stiff upper lip! Make hay while the sun shines, and remember, tomorrow is another day! Thank you, Scarlett O'Hara!

Metamorphosis

When a friend dies, it's a quandary on what is just the right thing to say or do...Through the years, I have found it really doesn't matter what I say or do. It just doesn't matter, as long as I do something!

It's the gentle touching of my spirit to a friend's grieving spirit that matters. Being there or sending a card shows I care, and brings warmth to a shattered soul. Saying "I wish you a Blessed Journey." This is such a gentle way to be there for my grieving friend.

Do you know why earthling angels have just one wing? That way their spirits can soar by embracing each other. Our human spirits are indomitable!

In my life there have been times to give heartfelt gifts and times to receive these special gifts.

More than a little rain has fallen in my life. (In fact, I've faced a few tsunamis)!

Always I've told my grandchildren, "Gran is a Guardian Angel in Training. God doesn't think I'm ready yet, but when my time comes, a special bell will ring and Gran will get her wings. It will be my time to *Light Beam to Heaven*!"

Precious

The most precious things in this world can neither be touched or seen. They must be felt by the heart. A heart smile is so personally charming. The dictionary defines the heart as “a hollow muscular organ that pumps the blood throughout the body by contracting and dilating.”

There is so much more to my heart. My heart glows with ethereal radiance, which enchants me, while doing its very human mission of pumping blood.

Unexpectedly, I will hear a lovely old song play and my heart will smile, sending a sentimental curve to my lips and a twinkle to my eyes.

Other times I'll only hear the beginning notes. It will be like a warming fire on the hearth on a cold snowy night; a song that was "Our Song" so many years ago. This is joy personified for me!

Another time of personal joy is when I'm reading and one word jumps right off the page, zooming straight to my heart and says, "That's it!" A word from the past or a new one that is just perfect for the situation.

Nostalgia sends my heart on a journey evoking simple pleasures of my long life. Locked away memories of my youth burst forth with a gentle nudge from an old song's melody. They are "a zinger" to my sentimental heart and a treasure trove of precious times gone by. My beating heart is a crescendo of happiness. This is the pure essence of joy when "these notes" or "that one word" burst forth leaving me with a happy smile and dancing eyes. Times of precious memories are what it means to be A Lady of a Certain Age. Precious!

Easter Dinner?

A glorious Easter Sunday dawned bright with sunshine and warm breezes. The first spring robins were chirping, and the tulips and daffodils were in full bloom. It was the perfect storybook Easter Sunday.

My family had gathered in Santa Fe for our Easter Soiree. Our daughter, Kim, and her family are always gracious hosts. The table was aglow with Easter trappings and We Ladies of a Certain Age appreciated the time it took to make the house look like Easter.

The meal was delicious! We laughed, told tall tales, and I had a chance to read excerpts from my book. Everyone laughed, which made me happy. What I am trying to do is make We Ladies of a Certain Age relish the humor in our lives.

We were lingering at the dining room table. Our times together are Oh…so precious!

The sun was getting low in the sky, and we all were gazing out the picture windows. The lovely rainbow glimmer from the water fountain, and the spring greenery kept us very mellow enjoying the moment.

When what to our wandering eyes should appear, but the beloved family kitty with a large bunny in his mouth!

Horror of horrors! We were appalled and riveted to the scene unfolding! In unison, we all yelled, "Sugar is about to eat the Easter bunny." Well…not quite! Sugar was so shocked by our reaction to his Easter dinner he ran away, dropping the surprised bunny, who…hippity-hopped into the sunset! Not everyone had their Easter dinner!

Missing "Ma Bell"

I don't think there is one of "we oldies" that don't have a pang in our hearts for that plain black telephone that rang "Riinnnggg." The house phone was so dependable and the family perked up when they heard that "Riinnnggg." (I wonder Whom it's for)? Yes, someone really wanted to talk with one of us! Then if you were a kid, you could only talk for just so long, freeing up the phone for another call. "Ma Bell" was always so dependable, and we took her for granted!

Pay phones directly outside of special stores were a wonder and a local call only cost

25c. Then there were phone booths seemingly to be placed randomly. I think we all thought this was as far as this modern invention could go…but fast forward to the twenty-first century…Behold the "I" phone. It's almost super human. "Look, Ma, no hands." Plus, you can play music, take pictures, ask directions, etc. Truly we were born in an age of miracles!

Grandpa Charlie

My father-in-law, Charlie Finley, was a great inspiration for me in unexpected ways. Everybody loved him, and he died at the ripe old age of ninety-seven. Charlie had a remarkably active mind at ninety-seven, and he made me laugh at his old time stories and observations on modern day life. (I was watching TV with him when Neil Armstrong landed on the moon).

One evening when we were watching the news, a segment came on about Jesse James being shot on the railroad platform in North-Field Minn. Charlie calmly announced,

"Yeah, I was there on that platform and saw the whole thing!" My family was all dumbfounded that Grandpa Charlie was really *that old*. He had been six years old when he saw Jesse James shot, and at ninety-seven years old, he remembered it vividly.

Another eye-opener for me about growing old was one morning when we were getting ready to drive to town from the lake. Walking to the car was no problem, but getting Charlie's legs in the passenger's side was troublesome. Finally achieving the position he wanted, Charlie gave his legs a slap and said, "Damned old body I'm trapped in!" It was then I realized the elderly are not a different species but antique young people. I was only twenty-eight at the time. Realizing an old person's mind is the sum total of their entire life was profound. What a blessed life's journey Charlie was on.

Along the way, this charming older gentleman still strived for a meaningful lifestyle. He had worked hard, made a good living, and surrounded himself with like-minded people. He married our "Gran Beezie" late in life. This gave our family a new grandpa and a preview of our future.

Now...what was the fuel that kept Charlie at ninety-seven loving life? He never heard the word *organic*, *diet*, or *exercise*. Charlie just ate what he liked, and it kept him happy and healthy. He did like to walk along the lake shore at sunset.

Charlie's diet was pretty routine. Breakfast always consisted of two fried eggs, four slices of bacon, orange juice, toast, and two cups of coffee with two lumps of sugar and a dash of cream. Charlie could always eat what he wanted, no restrictions. Lunch was a sandwich, usually ham or roast beef, with chips, cookies, fruit, and milk to drink. (I never saw him drink water)? Charlie wasn't a "snacker," but before dinner drank two scotch and sodas, smoked a couple of Camel cigarettes, and watched Walter Cronkite on the TV.

In the summer, my family always visited Beezie and Charlie at Lake Okoboji. When visiting, it was a treat to dine with them every night. The food was delicious. For the main course we usually ate friend chicken from the farm, Iowa beef, or freshly caught fish. Vegetables (Iowa corn and beans) were local and we all loved ice cream for dessert. Charlie always ate well and so did we.

Sometimes, for a special treat for dinner, Charlie made his famous dollar-sized pancakes. They were yummy! I can't decide whether watching him flip them or observing the twinkle in his eye was more fun.

Always, Charlie served his pancakes with plenty of real butter and real maple syrup. On the side, he served his special sausage. Never would he tell his secret ingredients.

The family all treasured Grandpa Charlie, and we missed him when he died. At his funeral, we met his two older sisters for the first time. The girls were 103 and 105 years old. Midwesterners are a hearty bunch!

Mystery Markets

To market…to market…to be surprised by the mystery foods of the day! Some taste great and are good for me, and others I tolerate, i.e., *Kale and Goji Beans*!

Remember when wheat was the staff of life, and pasta was called spaghetti. Every family made their own spaghetti sauce and nobody ever heard of pizza (unless you lived in an Italian neighborhood).

We paid attention to the food pyramid, which the new millennium has turned upside down…Sort of the same concept as do you put a baby to sleep on his (her) back, tummy, or side? Really, it doesn't matter!

Having diverted from my subject matter, I am now strolling through produce, which is an eye-opener! Iceberg lettuce used to be it! Now the varieties are staggering: romaine, butter, mixed spring greens, baby spinach, and *kale*, etc.

Crossing the aisle to fresh fruit is educational. What used to be apples, pears, peaches, with melons, grapes, and berries in season, now are new offerings: Goji beans, beautiful red and green Dragon fruit nestled in between, the hybrids, Nectaplums, Plumerries, and Pluots. All of them are delicious. I also saw an Indian butter melon, which looked good enough to eat!

When I was a child, Idaho potatoes and new potatoes were it. Now there's Yukon gold, fingerling, sweet potatoes, and yams. (Do you know the difference)?

Glancing over at the vegetables, I am amazed! Whoever heard of purple broccoli? It looks positively un-American!

Do you remember when homogenized milk was a *big deal*? If we bought whole milk, mother would pour the cream off the top into a creamer to save for our breakfast cereal. Now look at the variety of milk which has jumped right next to our traditional cow's milk. There is almond and coconut milk, kefir, and an assortment of organic, low fat, and lactose free. The choices are staggering!

My favorite milk of all time was unpasteurized. It came from Mackelhanies Dairy here in Albuquerque and was bought by the gallon in returnable glass bottles. (We poured the cream off the top for cereal, and it always tasted so fresh and delicious) Our children grew up drinking Mackelhanie milk, and they looked forward to the drive each week to visit the dairy.

Heading off to the cereal shelves, I am amazed with the variety! What used to be Corn Flakes, Rice Krispies, Cheerios, and all the "kid stuff" are now joined by Swiss Museli, Puffed Millet, Veganic Brown Crisps, and the big three: Quinoa, Couscous, and Kasha. Kasha used to be called Buckwheat in days of yore!

Nowadays, the in thing is to go vegan! But I notice some pretty good-looking steaks and hamburger in the meat department. Chops, roasts, and poultry look delicious, too, but I'm not sure about ground buffalo and ostrich?

Fish has been a staple since Bibical times, and we humans continue to be "fish eaters."

There are a few weird additions out there: Calamari (tubes and tentacles) etc. Then Tilapia isn't weird, but what is it? There was no Tilapia swimming around when I was a girl, just Trout, Catfish, Tuna, and Whitefish from Lake Superior.

Everybody loves seafood. Yumm! Delicious Lobster, Shrimp, and Crab are still out there, but mighty pricey!

All in all, it's fun exploring the modern-day markets, and most of the remarkable new foods are delicious. Try them! We're never too old to savor the exotic tastes of the new millennium.

Spackling

Sticks and stones can break my bones…but words will never hurt me! Walk, softly, but carry a big stick!

Don't make a mountain out of a molehill! Don't cut off your nose to spite your face or jump from the frying pan into the fire!

Look before you leap…Step on a crack, you'll break your mother's back!

Children should be seen and not heard… The squeaky wheel gets the grease!

A man is known by the company he keeps… Birds of the same feather flock together!

Why does a chicken cross the road? To get to the other side! Don't count your chickens before they've hatched!

You can't kill two birds with one stone…A bird in the hand is worth two in the bush!

When the cat's away, the mice will play… Every dog has his day!

Mind your manners and keep a stiff upper lip! Be a good listener, so you don't put your foot in your mouth!

(Sidebar to supper time).

Mother always said when I choked, "Did it go down your Sunday throat?" "Chew with your mouth shut and keep your elbows off the table…" "Don't gangplank your knife and fork and make sure you keep your napkin in your lap!"

Little pitchers have big ears…Think before you speak! It's always darkest right before the dawn! Arise and greet the morning…Early to bed, early to rise, makes a man healthy, wealthy, and wise! The early bird gets the worm!

It's a long road that has no turning! Bloom where you are planted!

Don't take life too seriously it isn't permanent!

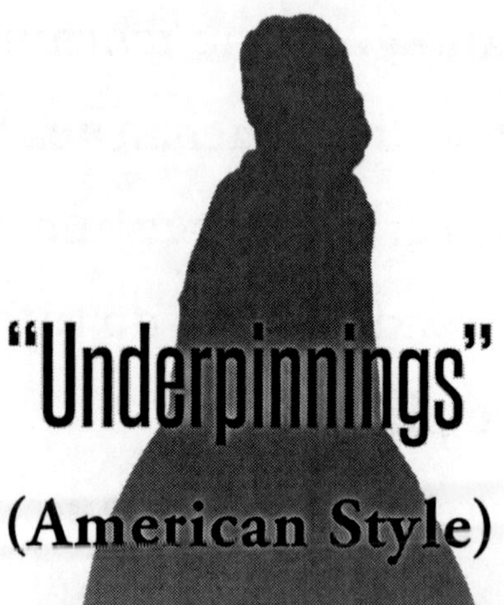

"Underpinnings"

(American Style)

My first Sortie! into underpinnings was at a very young age. My mother, after deliberating, took me to see *Gone with the Wind*, Margaret Mitchell's epic Civil War drama. The movie was eye-opening for this young girl.

The heartwarming, humorous part of the movie was the relationship between teen-age Scarlett and her beloved Mammy. I was amused by the scene when Scarlett was hanging on to the bedpost while Mamee tightened the laces on her corset. This was an eye-opener for me and a glance into the female foibles of looking fabulous!

Mammy was both devoted and bossy, while Scarlett was headstrong and somewhat a spoiled brat. She took all of Mammy's fussing, with that outraged glare of a wronged teenager! From the late 1860s—We have come a long way, Baby!

Fast-forward to the Roaring Twenties—"Flappers," as young ladies were called, danced till dawn having shed the proper underpinnings of the 1880s. It was fun, fun, fun in their most skimpy chemise, fringed dresses, and newly bobbed hairdos. The dances of the day were the Charleston and the Black Bottom (Is that politically Correct)?

What helped this party spirit along was "bathtub gin" and looking Oh! So! Glamorous! To complete the ambiance, young ladies casually held unlit cigarettes in their exquisite cigarette holders awaiting "a light" from their special beau. It was prohibition and the country was "busting loose" in frivolity.

From "Boom to Bust," the 1929 stock market "Crash" brought the country to its knees for the 1930's. This was a very sobering time, and the clothes reflected the mood of the country. House dresses were in and so were serious, drab underwear and slips. The corselet was worn by all; more comfortable than a corset. Some ladies wore a garter belt. (Not the sexy Fredrick's version of the future).

Stockings were in! Seamed silk was available if you could afford them, but cotton stockings were worn by most. It was tacky, but some ladies knotted their stockings below the knee with elastic!

On to the '40s and the war years. World War II made silk stockings sparse as the silk was needed for parachutes, but voilà, miracle of miracles along came nylons, and we still relish their practicality in the new millennium.

The last quarter of the twentieth century presented some "pretties" for we Ladies "not yet" of a Certain Age. Sliding across our radar were half-slips, so we no longer had to wrestle with falling shoulder straps. Then there appeared "the waist cincher" and the "Merry Widow!" What a name for an apparatus that was all lace and bows and made your figure fabulous!

Now we graduated from the well-constructed, ugly braziers to the cute plaid bras for budding breasts and for those more endowed, the Playtex Living Bra, the lacy underwire bra, and the push-up bra (great for cleavage for small-busted beauties) appeared on the market.

Then horror of horrors the Playtex girdles came, and we all wore them to get that Marilyn Monroe figure. Ladies were packed to perfection with baby powder galore, and it was a wrestling match just getting the girdle on with its millions of tiny little holes for ventilation. The Playtex girdle was made of a rubberish fabric, reminiscent of the middle ages, Iron Maiden. What we wouldn't do for the sake of beauty! When we disrobed, we had to slither out of the sweaty contraption, while the tiny holes sucked your tender skin making little red marks. *Sidebar:* I laughed about Scarlett O'Hara having her corset laced—tight, tight, tight "Me thinks" we ladies any age are just a little nutty!

On to the millennium! We ladies bodies were truly liberated! The sports bra (thank you Mia Hamm) not so sexy but cute, and oh so comfortable! Then here came the thong (very sexy but not so comfortable), the exception being perfectly proportioned beauties announcing, "I just love my thongs they're so comfortable!"

Then the invention all ladies cheer for, Spandex. How did we exist without it? Just think what Scarlett O'Hara could have done with spandex and hip huggers, and it would have been Bye! Bye! Mamee!

P.S. I bet Scarlett would have relished having a naughty thong… and so would Rett!

Our Comedians

The era we are born in is, of course, the era we think produced the funniest and most endearing comedians. Being completely prejudiced, I know for sure the comedians performing in the 1940s, '50s, '60s, and '70s had the best "shtick!" No comedians have been better before or since. Just ask any Lady of a Certain Age.

These comedians owned the kaleidoscope of fun that was *really funny*! They didn't depend on biting sarcasm or lowdown nasty innuendos...(Maybe they got a little naughty around the edges)!

Carol Burnett…Who can ever forget her yanking down the forest green velvet drapes to portray Scarlett in *Gone with the Wind*! I'm laughing still thinking of that curtain rod slung across her shoulders, draping the green velvet curtains. Such dignity Carol exemplified as she strolled down that magnificent staircase! A real hoot!

Other comedic skits I remember are the hilarious antics of Lucille Ball and Vivian Vance. Remembering those two, stomping around in a vat of grapes, making wine was hilarious! Another of their priceless skits took place in a chocolate factory. The conveyer belt was too fast for them, so to keep up, they kept stuffing their mouths with chocolates! What gifted humor Lucille Ball and Vivian Vance had!

Now, who could forget Lily Tomlin with her "one ring-a-dingy, two ring-a-dingy?"

The men of our era were really funny, too. There was Harvey Coreman, who was so funny and laughed at his own antics on the Carol Burnett programs. Then there was Robin Williams, a unique talent. He was funny, funny, funny, but also a serious actor. You have got to see *Dead Poet's Society*!

Now for our "naughty boys!" Remember George Carlin cavorting with his dirty words! He always left me with an embarrassed, little chuckle. Two other naughty boys in our era were Red Foxx and Richard Pryor. Delightful irreverence!

Then there was our real American hero, Bob Hope. Always he will live in my heart! What a talented, funny guy Bob Hope was.

He was always there to entertain the troops, and he was loved by our nation!

There is a magnificent bronze statue of Bob Hope and his warriors. It is set in the most perfect place, on the shoreline of San Diego harbor. Memories are made of this!

The Human Spark

We Ladies of a Certain Age have all had fleeting moments with those very special strangers, who inadvertently have touched our lives. Their spark radiates, unknowingly from deep inside their souls. Their radiant glow catches our eye, never to be forgotten.

I am going to write about three of my never to be forgotten experiences. My first memory of the human spark was on my wedding day in 1954. That day I was overjoyed to be marrying Jack and felt very beautiful dressed in a lovely embroidered organdy wedding gown. I wore a fingertip veil and around my neck a dainty pearl necklace, which I since have had copied for my three granddaughters.

My wedding day, I was feeling nostalgic as my father had died when I was eight. When mother opened our apartment door I stepped into the corridor and my nostalgic heart was warmed. What an unexpected surprise to see all the employees of our apartment hotel lining the corridor. They just stood there with radiant smiles on their faces. They had come to give me a sendoff on my way to the church.

Not one of them spoke. It was their eyes that spoke, their tender looks never to be forgotten! I never knew their names but had always been polite and spoke kindly to them. Word must have spread that it was my wedding day and this was their gift.

This outpouring of good will from virtual strangers has stayed with me all of my life. I wonder if they knew how much their heartfelt tribute meant to me and that I would always remember.

My second memory of the human spark was in the lobby of the University of New Mexico hospital. Walking through the revolving doors, into the lobby, I came across a tiny stooped lady pushing her grown son in a very large wheelchair. As I watched them, I caught the look in their eyes when they smiled at each other. That look they had for each other was the essence of Heavenly Joy. "No Greater Love."

I noticed before moving on that everyone else in the lobby was standing stark still with me as the mother and son moved on. We were witnessing devotion and love personified. Their eyes! Never will I forget!

My third experience with the human spark was on a bitter cold day at a car wash. I was shivering waiting for my car to be dried and thinking I was so blessed not to be working in a car wash!

When the man finished, I gave him a dollar. He looked me in the eye and said, "Bless you, Lady." I have never felt so blessed in my life! To this day I wonder who this man was?

Wake Island

The year was 1959. Jack, my husband, was a dashing young Air Force pilot, and I was Jack's devoted wife. My time was spent "wrangling" our two babies with Jack's help! Kim was almost two and Johnny was almost one. (Birth control pills were not yet on the market).

Jack was due for an overseas tour of duty, and we were excited pondering the places (he or we) could be stationed. We were ecstatic when Jack's orders came through for a four-year accompanied tour to Tachikawa Air Force Base, Japan.

It was a "win-win" assignment. Jack *would fly*, we'd be together, and we could have a house with a live-in maid! Wow! It was time to celebrate!

We were to fly from San Francisco to Tokyo on a prop-driven airplane. In 1959, this flight took thirty-six hours. It was going to be a *doozy* traveling with our babies, but Jack and I were young and undaunted. Jack was twenty-four, Lloyda was twenty-two, and what an adventure we were about to embark on!

We boarded our flight, babies in tow, armed with several dozen clean but ragged diapers from the diaper service (disposables hadn't been invented yet) and of course a caboodle of Gerber's baby food went, too.

Marines. Our fellow travelers turned out to be just that, forty-eight young Marines headed unaccompanied to Tokyo. We were the only family on board. Thirty-six hours is a l-o-n-g time with babies on an airplane, but *SEMPER FI*! These young Marines took the challenge. They played with Kim and Johnny and made the trip just plain fun for all of us.

When our airplane landed on Wake Island to refuel, Marines and Albach family were ready for a break. The Marines hightailed it to the telephones and snack bar, while Jack and I headed for the beach, babies in tow. As we arrived on the shore, dawn broke in all its South Pacific Splendor. We were mesmerized by what lay before us!

In the surf, not far from shore, lay two gigantic American Destroyers, terminally wounded relics of a disastrous sea battle in World War II.

These stately ships had mangled hulls and gaping holes in their sides. Here their wounds had lain exposed since that fateful day during World War II when they had been fatally torpedoed by the Japanese navy.

Our once mighty destroyers still endured! The azure blue waves undulated past, soothing their wounds before sweeping onto the sandy shore.

Jack and I were speechless! Our babies wanted *down…now*! So we set them in the warm South Pacific Sea. Joy, oh! Joy for Kim and Johnny. They giggled and cooed as their tiny hands patted the sunlight reflections in the waves which raced to meet the shore.

For Jack and me, this was a hallowed time, a time for introspection. The future and the past were with us! We were not clearly in *then*, nor were we in the *now*.

At the time, I don't think either one of us realized the impact this early morning interlude on Wake Island would have on our lives. It became our tale of The South Pacific written down by Lloyda more than half a century after World War II.

God Bless those men who died that day! May their families have a blessed journey in life and know always they will live in our tale of the South Pacific.

From the Mist of Time

Like Jams and Jellies here are sayings good enough to preserve.

1-Don't be a spent force!

2-Keep a stiff upper lip!

3-Wopse.... it went down my Sunday throat!

4-Don't air your dirty laundry in public!

5-It's darkest right before the dawn!

6-What a Ko-Hinky-Dinky that was!

7-She's full of spit and vinegar!

8-Keep your knees crossed, you'll stay out of trouble!

9-If you look like a Great Dane don't act like a French Poodle!

10-Always wear CLEAN underwear! (You might be in an accident)!

11-I've got a frog in my throat!

12-Stop acting like you're the bride at the wedding and the corpse at the funeral!

13-Don't trouble trouble, till trouble troubles you!

14-Keep your shoulders back (Knockers up) Chin up, look people in the eye!

15-If it looks like a duck, quacks like a duck… it's a duck!

16-If you have fallen into a pile of "Horse Hockey" there has to be a pony somewhere!

Be a good listener! (I'm really trying now I'm in my eighties)!

The Howl

On a haunted summer's eve, evolving into a murky, black night, a coyote pack gathers for their evening hunt. From Sandia Mountain, they come down my arroyo, slinking one by one as they track their doomed prey. Just behind my garden wall, the coyotes *stop*… and…stealthily circle their victim. Patiently, they wait for the kill until the moon and stars are shrouded by dark, dank clouds. Evil is afoot, and the night air seethes with eminent shock!

While this scenario unfolds, my pets and I are calmly getting ready for bed. We become restless. Penetrating the light summer breeze wafting through the bedroom window, an unexpected aura of tension and foreboding swirls around the room.

After a period of tossing and turning, we cozy up and slept peacefully until "The Howl" shatters our slumber! My pets all dive under the covers while I sit bolt upright, bug-eyed, hackles rising on the back of my neck. The unison howl from the coyote pack, closing in on their prey is straight from hell! Being completely immobilized by unearthly sound, the prey never knew what hit it, and a merciful meal was devoured by the coyote pack.

"The Howl," always earsplitting, happens once in a Blue Moon! It's not something man or beast ever gets used to. The harrowing, unison howling from the coyote pack always brings a chilling fear to my heart. In reflection, this Lady of a Certain Age is blessed to live in a warm, safe home. There are advantages having been born in 1934 instead of 1834.

Think of the pioneer wives traveling west in a covered wagon on a haunting night when they were rudely awakened by "The Howl."

My New Neighbors

Living in the foothills of Sandia Peak, I have become accustomed to seeing wildlife on my walks. Bears come down in the fall forging for fruit. The deer sashay down the street sampling the most delectable summer flowers. An occasional bobcat shows up and once a huge mountain lion.

Who has captured my heart is a rather small female coyote, who moved into my neighborhood. She lives in the arroyo behind my house under a protecting ledge.

There she has given birth to three coyote pups. My coyote is such a good mother, and the pups are endearing. I watch, but never get close to her or her pups.

My heart is rent because I don't want her to eat my pets. This was coyote land before it was mine, and I respect this.

The other day while gazing out my front window, here she came herding her pups. I know she saw me in the window and dropped her pups in my front yard while she went to get a drink in the neighbor's fish pond.

The pups romped in the grass in my front yard. In a very short time, she came back to take them for their drink and then herded them back down the cut into the arroyo to their home.

I admire my new neighbors, but they are unsettling.

Gifts

Pre-dawn is special for this Lady of a Certain Age! The morning bird's song signals the beginning of another day. I'm still here, and every day is a special occasion! It is a gift!

By evening, I relish the surprises in my day. Sunsets always dazzle this mortal's imagination. As sunset transforms to that mystical vesper light, I am enchanted by earth's heavenly grandeur.

As velvet black night falls with its star-studded sky, I anticipate the ever-changing phases of the moon. What a gift!

These gifts of nature sustain me! Hardly a week goes by I don't get "the call." I just wanted to let you know…I steel myself to hear about another good friend who's earned (his/her) wings!

What heartbreak these calls bring. Watching my generation (including me) fade is mind-boggling!

Yes, I'm sad, but then that little voice in my heart pipes up and says, "Remember, you are a Guardian Angel in training, and God isn't ready for you yet!"

It's time to bring out my kaleidoscope of humor and happy memories! Being planted loosely in two centuries, I thank God for the gift of another day! My life is a closer walk with God, and yes! God does have a plan!

The Ladies of La Vida Llena

Nestled near the foothills of the Sandia Mountains in Albuquerque, New Mexico, lies an enchanted retirement community, La Vida Llena. It is a beautiful setting and those who live there have channeled their resources to live a stimulating life with like-minded souls.

I have found these ladies to be rugged individuals, fascinating to visit with. Their popery of backgrounds and unpretentious manner intrigue me. All these ladies are individuals with a common thread. Regardless of their advanced age, they are vital, still wanting to grow, develop, and cherish each new day.

It is astounding how the ladies lives intersected with important historical moments of the twentieth century. Being in a measured time of life they exhibit remarkable spunk and gumption with a ready smile and a twinkle in their eye. These ladies' days are precious, and they exemplify generosity of spirit. It is a true blessing to have the opportunity of knowing them.

It makes me smile to think of myself as a La Vida Llena legacy. My charismatic, feisty mother-in-law was one of the first residents when La Vida Llena opened its doors in 1983. Beezie was a love of a person but took a dim view of moving into La Vida Llena. She called it *the poor farm*! Grudgingly, she moved in to please her son, and surprisingly after only a week she was hooked, being completely engaged with her new home. In fact, she was the "Go to Person" for management to take along when showing prospective residents around. Beezie was safe and had her independence, and Jack and I had peace of mind.

To learn more about this resilient group, you may read Turning Ponts, Volume I and II. The stories are poignant and fascinating. Each lady in her own way has made her splash in life and is living the ripple.

INTERMISSION

(No pretty Music Will Play)

BUT

YOU MAY READ

The Favorites

A sweet glimpse into the Seasons,

which compose a lifetime

Read on… Ladies!

Prologue to Favorites

When formulating thoughts on my Favorite Time of Year, I planned to elaborate on just one season. After pondering, my thoughts skipped around to all the seasons, and I found I loved them all! This new love threw a monkey wrench in my original plan!

So I ended my story plan wanting to honor just one season! Each one has its endearing charm! My mind wandered recalling just what made each season so special. They were the seasons of my life!

So here…here come all those favorite times with lots of Bang, Sparkle and Pop! I love them all—winter, spring, summer, and fall. Isn't that fitting for A Lady of a Certain Age!

I hope my writing will awaken your heart's memory to the treasured years gone by. Happy reading to my fellow travelers!

My Favorite Time of The Year

New Year's

"Should Auld Acquaintance be forgot and never brought to mind, should Auld Acquaintance be forgot and days of Auld Lang Syne." It's a kiss good-bye to the old year and a champagne toast to the new!

Of course, New Year's is my favorite time of the year! To make it more special for me, it's my birthday (1-2-34). *Really!* It's the time for new beginnings, resolutions, with love and laughter, high hopes and good will!

My New Year's Day joy is watching the annual Rose Bowl parade televised from Pasadena, California. Such an all-American tradition. The magnificence of the floats represent the untold hours of work from the many volunteers, tirelessly working with only fresh flowers and their imaginations. The creations are truly an act of love producing eye popping floral splendor!

The parade starts with a thundering fly-over complete with sonic boom. Then here comes the Rose Bowl queen, the marching bands, the colorful horses interspersed with the magnificent floats.

I always say, "This year was the most beautiful parade!" This day is America at its showy best, and the parade I just watched was The Most Beautiful!

My Favorite Time of The Year
Valentine's Day

Valentine's Day is for lovers! Of course it is my favorite time of the year! I still send Valentine cards from the Dollar Store to those folks that are closest to my heart. The messages on these Dollar Store cards are always right on the mark, perfect!

Valentine's Day is such a sweet holiday, yum! Does anyone ever turn down a frilly box of chocolates? Not me! Roses are red, violets are blue, sugar is sweet, and so are you!

I love the multitude of red roses that abound in the stores as Valentine's Day draws near. When I receive a bouquet, they come straight from cupid's arrow! What a loving tradition!

Yes, all in all, Valentine's Day is my favorite time of the year. My most decadent delights are the chocolate-covered strawberries, yum! Happy Valentine's Day to you!

My Favorite Time of The Year-
St. Patrick's Day

Hurrah for the wearing of the green! It's St. Patrick's Day, my favorite time of the year! You'll hear Irish sayings like "Top of the morning to you," and then you may go looking for a four-leaf clover. It's the one time of the year to make corned beef and cabbage and drink green beer. St. Paddy's day is full of fun, tradition, and pranks. If I were in Ireland, I would kiss the Blarney Stone and sing "My Wild Irish Rose." Isn't everybody Irish on St. Patrick's Day? To celebrate, try this traditional St. Paddy's Day recipe from my Irish great-grandmother's recipe box:

St. Patty's Soup
For Loopy Leprechauns

7 Cups Water- 3Ibs. Corned Beef- ½ C Chopped Onion- 2 Whole Cloves- 1 Bay Leaf- 2 Cloves Garlic – 6 Pepper Corns- 2 Beef Bouillon Cubes-1 Tsp. Instant Bouillon-1/2 package Baby Carrots and 6 Cups Coarsely Chopped Cabbage.

In a Dutch Oven or Crock Pot pour 7 Cups Water – bring to a boil after adding 3Ibs. Corned Beef – Skim off Scum. Then add ½ Chopped Onion-2 Whole Cloves-1 Bay Leaf-2 Cloves Garlic- 6 Pepper Corns-2 Beef Bouillon Cubes and 1 Tsp. Instant Bouillon.

Simmer on low 4 hours till tender- Remove Meat-Skim fat-Cut Meat in bite size pieces-Return to Broth-Add ½ package Baby Carrots-6 cups Chopped Cabbage- Bring to boil and then let simmer for 15 mins. Remove Pepper Corns, Garlic Cloves, serves approximately 10-Freezes well!

My Favorite Time of The Year

Easter

Springtime puts on its own Easter parade! It is my favorite time of the year when my cherry tree blossoms snow-white pedals, and my apple trees bloom in shades of pink and mauve. It is heaven right here on earth! The air smells so sweet, and the breezes rustle through my lovely trees dressed for spring.

It's spring! The birds have arrived back in my yard, and it's time for them to build their nests. It's a busy time for the birds, and I welcome them to my trees.

Soon, I will start looking for Hermione, my fascinating hummingbird. She is a real "snow bird" and has been wintering in South America. Her nest on my iron trellis has made it through the winter and awaits her return.

The greening of my lawn and the leafing of my trees are God's gift to spring and me. The flowers are blooming in my yard and all over town. They are so pretty to behold. Hearts are lighter and there is joy in the air. Welcome spring, most definitely, my favorite time of the year!

P.S. Hermione just arrived back from South America. She now cares for two tiny hatchlings named Steve and Lilly.

My Favorite Time of The Year
Memorial Day

Like rosemary for remembrance, Memorial Day is so reflective. It is my favorite time of the year! This day lives in memory each year in the private parts of my sentimental heart.

So many souls, whom I have loved in my lifetime, live on in my memory. The spring of the year infuses my being with memories of springs and summers past.

Have you ever been honored to attend a funeral at Arlington Cemetery? It is our National Cemetery and a hallowed resting place of honor. Experiencing Arlington lives in my heart forever.

Witnessing the changing of the guard at the tomb of the Unknown Soldier sent shivers up and down my spine and tears to my eyes. Such patriotic magnificence…a Tribute!

Continuing on to the burial sight of our fallen friend, I was overwhelmed with pride for our brave fallen heroes. As the horse-drawn caisson passed mile after mile of snow-white gravestones, I was infused by the honor and dignity of such a sad occasion.

Being laid to rest with his Band of Brothers was fitting. The twenty-one-gun salute was the final "goodbye" sent from his squadron and those who loved him dearly.

Yes, Memorial Day is my favorite time of the year. I remember! Joe Murphy and his family: Bev, Mark, Terry, and Michael!

My Favorite Time of The Year

4th of July

The corn is knee high on the 4th of July, and it's time to celebrate my favorite time of the year, Independence Day! It's time for fireworks (the big flashy ones the city puts on and my beloved backyard display). I will always love those gunpowder snakes you light on a rock and they coil in crazy ways. Then of course the sparklers, so pretty, which are the first fireworks the children learn to hold. The night is filled with celebrating sounds, and its Happy Birthday, USA.

The Fourth of July is a day of picnics and splashing in the water; lakes, rivers, or swimming pools. From the time we were children, the diet of the day is hamburgers, hot dogs, watermelon, and s'mores!

It's time to wave the flag, go to Fourth of July parades and thank God for our luck in having been born in the greatest country in the world! Hurrah for the United States of America!

When the canons go off at the end of the "William Tell Overture," I cheer and salute in my heart… My Country 'tis of Thee Sweet Land of Liberty…and it's the only one in the world!

My Favorite Time of The Year
Labor Day

Labor Day…Let's Celebrate! It's time to jump into fall, my favorite time of the year! Brightly colored leaves begin fluttering off the trees, and the air has that nip to it. It's the start of the school year, and its fun watching the little children board the big yellow school bus for the first time. This sight always brings a nostalgic glimmer to my eye.

It's "YEA" for the moms! They survived another summer of "Mommy! Mommy! M-o-m-m-e-e-e!" After the summer games, picnics, and water sports, it's farewell to the sun splashed days of summer and welcome, Labor Day, the harbinger of fall.

As we put summertime to bed, it's time to plan for the Labor Day picnic, the last hurrah of summer!

Now is the time for new endeavors. In the background of morning breezes the music from the newly formed high school marching bands waft through the air. The notes are crisp and clear with brisk sounds that signify fall.

It is football and soccer and lots of fall projects, and time to embrace it all. Fall, my favorite time of the year!

My Favorite Time of The Year

Halloween

Boo! It's spooky Halloween, All Hallows Eve, the night before All Saints Day! Ghosts and goblins abound! Both young and old are out on the town seeking tricks or treats. Being a witch of a certain age, of course, makes Halloween my favorite time of the year!

The myriad carved jack-o'-lanterns announce the most fun day of the year has finally arrived! The littlest of the ghosts and goblins are the most adorable when they arrive at the front door begging treats. Such polite little monsters!

There is a little *kid* in all of us on Halloween! Whether it is decorating the yard or giving a party, it's a hilarious time of year. My favorite outside decoration is the "Ditsy Witch" riding her broomstick smack into a Telephone pole. There she is legs askew, arms flaying, broom stick in hand, hanging on for dear life! Watch for her on Halloween. This "Ditsy Witch" really is that funny!

Living in New Mexico, we have a delightful old-time Mexican tradition we have adopted. It's called Diá de los Muertos, translated "The Day of the Dead." It's a festive celebration partying away with our dearly departed ancestors.

With the vivid colors of fall surrounding us and snow clouds gathering over Sandia Mountain, it's time for magic! 'Tis the season to listen for things that go bump in the Night!

My Favorite Time of The Year
Thanksgiving Day

The leaves have all fluttered off the trees in an array of gold and red. The sun is still warm, but the wind is starting to chill and it's time to celebrate Thanksgiving, our very own American holiday! Yes, Thanksgiving is my favorite time of the year!

Our American tradition has come a long way since the Pilgrims landed on Plymouth Rock. The modern Thanksgivings are different than the ones our ancestors celebrated, but the original spirit of the holiday is still there, Thankfulness!

We still "Gather Together to ask the Lord's Blessing!" All families have their own special traditions with a heavy dose of football on the side. Remarkably, there are still plenty of elements of the old fashioned Thanksgiving that are celebrated year after year.

My Favorite Time of The Year

Christmas

"Sleigh bells ring are you listening?" Christmas carols are being played on my car radio. Hark! It's almost Christmas, my favorite time of the year! Every year we celebrate the birth of the baby Jesus. It's such a wonderful season, and we all celebrate in different ways. "Glory to God in the Highest, and Peace on Earth Good Will towards Men!"

The first gentle snow brings a twinkle to my eyes, and snowmen and snow angels say winter has arrived.

Arriving from our daughter, Kim, is an Advent Calendar just for me! What a smile this brings to my face as it shows the traditions of her childhood live on! "Yes, Virginia there is a Santa Claus!"

It's time to get out all the trappings for Christmas. Time to make traditional goodies and savor the scents (cinnamon, clove, pinon, and pine, the most enticing).

How dear my Christmas tree is as it glows brightly with tiny lights. The branches are elegantly laden with sentimental ornaments, some going back seventy-five years.

It's time to wrap the presents. I shop all year so now is the time to find the right shaped boxes and pretty bows. Gift bags really do help, but the Three Wise Men had the right idea with Gold, Frankincense, and Myrrh!

Finally, it's Christmas Eve. Time to light the Luminarias to welcome the Christ child (a lovely tradition here in New Mexico). Merry Christmas to all, and to all a good night!

A Family Favorite
Sweet Potatoes New Mexico Style

Good for Christmas
(Thanksgiving, too!)

4 Large Sweet Potatoes- 1 Stick Butter- Small Carton Sour Cream-Chopped, Roasted Hatch Green Chilies to Taste.

Rub Potato Skins with Butter-Bake 375 for 1 Hour- Cool Slightly- Slice in Half and Scoop Out Potatoes - Mash with Butter (Room Temp.) and Sour Cream. Stir in Green Chilies to Taste- Yummy! It's Easy, Different and a Favorite with Everybody! Keep in Warm Oven!

Sidebar to Christmas

The Christmas cards! Once such a joy to send and receive! Now, it is a bittersweet experience!

Here comes the mailman! It's always such fun to watch for him in late December, rather it was in days of yore! Now being A Lady of a Certain Age, it's risky business and can bring a jolt or two of reality to my heartstrings.

As I wave at the mailman and retrieve my Christmas cards, I notice a percentage in my own handwriting. *Wow!* How come? Where did my friends go? No forwarding address stamped on my cards means…moved to Assisted Living or Light Beamed to Heaven??

I guess there are no mail deliveries in the hereafter!

There is little Christmas cheer in those sweet notes written by my friend's relatives. They thank me for a lifetime of friendship I had shared with their mothers. I have even received pictures of my friend waving "Good-Bye." (I have mixed emotions over these pictures sent at Christmas)!

Christmas cards used to be sharing graduations, weddings, new babies, new jobs, and vacations. Now these cards can be a somber awakening on how far "Tempus has

F-U-G-I-T-E-D!"

Having accepted the reality that none of us are immortal, even me, I smile letting nostalgia wash over me. Fond memories of past friendships live on in us survivors, and it is time to cherish *just being*! Surprise! We made it through another year!

TRANSITIONING

From

Fun With The Favorites

To MAGIC

….Next Page, Please!

Magic

Oh my! I would love to go to my favorite V. W. Garage, Foreign Aide, to get my joints oiled. What luxury to have oiled joints and a few magic screws inserted for stability! These magic screws would be tightened down, just so, to give my limbs (the ladylike term for arms and legs) stability. Then…I would have the bounce of youth when I walk!

While I'm in the garage, I think it would be a good idea to get my chassis realigned…so much for fantasy land!

Back to reality…In lieu of a tune-up at my favorite garage, I will tell you how I keep my ol', ol' joints mobile.

Stretching is my secret weapon! I do activate my joints daily! Gentle, not strenuous does the trick for me!

Early morning is my time to exercise. Doing my stretches in the pool is a great way to start the day, and it makes me feel… righteous!

My other nod to exercise is daily walks with my dogs. (It's debatable whose walking whom)!

Delilah, my Diva, Dachshund, and Tim, my tiny, snow-white Maltese are my buddies. We three love this time together!

We enjoy walking. I listen to my iPod (a fabulous gift from my daughter, Kim). She brought me into the twenty-first century!

While Delilah and Tim christen every bush, and both take time to sniff every tantalizing spot only dogs know about, WE WALK!

Delilah and Tim have their "doggie friends," they greet wholeheartedly, and I have my "doggie people" I look forward to greeting every morning!

When I started this book, I vowed not to be "preachy," but here goes, I'm going to sin a little!

Exercise, in my opinion, is a must! What I do may not be right for you…but try to do something! It really is "use it or loose it time!" Any kind of movement is good! You choose! Your body will love you for it!!

Stir. . . Don't Shake My Chi

Why would A Lady of a Certain Age want to attempt *Tai Chi*? If I were Chinese, maybe... But to get exotic at my age seems a bit silly! To please my granddaughters, Samantha and J. J., I agreed to give it a whirl! Both young ladies are in the medical profession and thought Tai Chi would benefit my balance.

So...off I went to a Tai Chi Chih class. Much to my surprise, I loved it! The teacher and the movements spoke to my heart! I found out even though I am not Chinese, the force of Chi does flow gently through my body.

Tai Chi Chih transcends east to west in a lovely way. It is a gentle form of exercise, undemanding, concentrating not on strength but the discipline of spirit. I learned to balance my yin and yang (the negative and positive sides of my nature). The movements are soft, slow, exacting, and very relaxing. They leave me open to accepting the mysterious flow of the vital force of intrinsic energy known as Chi.

To practice Tai Chi Chih, I try to free my body and mind. The stance is relaxed with softly cupped hands and gently bent knees. Next, I slowly shift my weight in repetitive circular motions. The continuous movement in a circular fashion is imperative to integrating my mind, body, and emotions. The result of these delicate dance motions is the balance of my Chi energy. The names of these disciplines are so charming. My favorites are Bird Flaps its Wings, Daughter on the Mountaintop, and Cosmic Breath.

Like baby brother Mikey, on the old TV cereal commercial, I tried something new and I found I liked it! The expressions on my granddaughters' faces when I told them I liked Tai Chi mirrored big brother's expressions on the old TV commercial. Samantha and J. J. were surprised and delighted for me.

Tai Chi Chih, I didn't just like…*I love it!* Now…in my eighties, I am not shying away from trying new things! And incidentally any practice that has lasted three thousand years is worth checking into!

The Boys in the Hot Tub

Do you remember when you were a kid and played at the neighborhood playground? I do! It was just plain fun finding someone to teeter-totter with, take turns pushing each other on the swings, and digging in the sandbox.

Fast-forward seventy-five years!

I started going to a club I will call Devine Fitness, which has an Olympic pool and a fabulous hot tub. My insurance is Silver Sneakers, which allows me to use the facility for free. You can't beat free! My favorite time to exercise is 5:45 a.m., and it's a great way to start the day.

After swimming and exercising in the water for forty-five minutes, I feel positively virtuous and treat myself to fifteen minutes of "lolla-gaging" in the hot tub. Here I "kibitz" and laugh a lot with "The Boys." We no longer resemble our Baywatch counterparts, David Hasselhoff and Pamela Anderson, but we do have fun telling tall tales and making each other laugh. "The Boys" razz and tease each other and me, but nobody gets mad. All of us are survivors, quirky and creaky. We have all learned the importance of laughter and exercise. The variety of unexpected humor keeps us laughing. It's fun being greeted, "Lady Lloyda" or "Here Comes Trouble." Always there are welcoming smiles and mischievous looks. All of us manage to keep our joints in gear and our minds functioning. "The Boys" in the hot tub are young at heart and just plain fun. With our verbal sparring, we manage to keep ourselves vital. Meeting "The Boys in the Hot Tub" was a happy accident. Being a widow, I like telling my friends, "All the men in my life are in the hot tub." This always produces lots of laughter and no more questions.

I salute you "Boys in the Hot Tub." You start my day with a smile, a joyful thought, and a twinkle in my eye. Happiness unexpectedly found me on my early morning sojourn to the pool. The best way to cheer yourself up is to cheer someone else up. Thank you, "Boys in the Hot Tub." I am honored to call you my friends.

Want to be a Chippie?

What do you think of getting chipped? I look down at my left wrist now and it makes me look like I've escaped from the chain gang! And it's all necessary ID!

I have an ID for when I'm out and about, a band with a buzzer if I should fall at home, and then there's my big-faced watch I've always worn. (Joy OH! Joy it can glow in the dark)!

Now I could get back to just my watch if I were chipped. We chip our dogs and cats so they don't get lost. Why not us?

If a baby was chipped at birth, think how handy this would be for the police. No lost or kidnapped children, no Ladies of a Certain Age wandering into the sunset, no hikers somewhere in the mountains!

Remember when we thought bicycle and motorcycle helmets were a rather unnecessary protection? Look now how everybody wears them, and they don't feel silly.

Chipping is "a way out there something" to think about in 2018, but I bet someday it will be an accepted practice. Just you wait and see! Here's *tweeting* to you and how about a Snap Chat!

From Tiny Acorns

"From tiny acorns mighty oak trees grow." I love this idea, and it epitomizes how the Albuquerque International Balloon Fiesta grew to become the Premier Balloon Fiesta in the world.

In 1972, the love of ballooning for Ben Abruzo and Maxie Anderson sparked their plan. They took three giant balloons to Coronado shopping center to lift off for the amazement of the crowd. Thus was the small beginning for the gigantic Albuquerque International event.

Today, in the Land of Enchantment, the Balloon Fiesta is the treasured gift from these two Albuquerque pioneer balloonists.

Tourists from around the world come to Albuquerque the first week in October. The skies are filled with the colorful majesty of the balloons floating in the crisp morning air. Foreigners and natives alike are filled with joy watching the giants of the sky.

It never grows old for us New Mexicans. The variety! The shapes! The colors! Up, up, and away the myriad shapes and colors rise on the cool early morning air, triggering a happy spot in all the onlookers' hearts.

To have watched these giants inflate is somewhat of a mystery. They have a spontaneous love affair with a crowd perplexed by the inert masses of color on the ground. Slowly, they come alive inflated by propane gas. As the crowd stands next to them in awestruck wonder, men dressed as zebras gently guard the balloons and the mesmerized onlookers.

The moment a balloon lifts off is to be held precious. There is an infinite relationship between those left standing on the ground and the newly soaring balloonists. The crowd feels part of what went into the ascension. A joyful part of the crowd's heart lifts off with the balloons.

The special shapes are so whimsical to watch. It's a time for wide-eyed wonder, awe, and enchantment.

Balloon glow magic lights the field in the evening. The balloons are tethered and illuminated so the crowd can appreciate the unique shapes. It's a magical stroll through fantasy, balloon land. Whether you are two or ninety-two, the glorious sight is reflected in the onlookers' eyes.

A Tribute

Dr. Rounds is my "Man for all Seasons." He has been my doctor for over twenty years, and I am truly blessed! His caring nature spills over to his office staff and is welcomed by his patients. No matter what the problem, Dr. Rounds is there for us with a twinkle in his eye!

What a treasure of a doctor he is! Truly I am thankful! I think Dr. Rounds truly tries to keep "his flock" from getting hoisted on their own Petards!

I am one of those "lucky ducks" able to keep "my" doctor, truly, I am thankful! It's costing me to stay with him, but if I don't have my health, nothing else matters! It's fun to kid him saying, "I'm not sure you're worth the extra dollars?" He assures me he is!

Dr. Rounds specializes in "heart smiles." My really good doctor is always there for me. When my husband, Jack, was dying, Dr. Rounds was my light in the dark. He was always a telephone call away from being with us medically and spiritually. Periodically, I would get a call in the evening just to see how we were doing. The really good doctors just know! This kind of devotion is not learned in a book; it's a partnership with the *man* upstairs.

Dr. Rounds's life is never truly his own (except on Wednesday afternoon when he plays golf)! His wife is a saint, and his children grew up learning what it means to have a doctor father. The God-like responsibility is mind-boggling.

I like to call Dr. Rounds, "The Wort Wizard" and his staff "His Coven." The small wort on my thumb, that persists in coming back, never do I let him forget! He is very good-natured about my title for him, but I'm sure he doesn't view himself as "The Wort Wizard!"

Thinking of Dr. Rounds makes me smile! What a good man! Just knowing he's there makes me feel safe and ready to take on each new day. Dr. Rounds is *my doctor*, and I would never call him Roger. The title Dr. Rounds just fits him!

My doctor is a consummate "patient person" with the exception of his Wednesday afternoon golf game. Someday, many moons from now, I imagine he will tee off through the

Pearly Gates, but until then, it's eat right and live well! By doing this, he expects us to love the gift of each new day. I make Dr. Rounds laugh, and he makes me, me. It's a mutual admiration society, and here I am writing a tribute to *my doctor*!

H_2O

To drink or not to drink, that is the question? I am not talking about imbibing of the grape but plain ol' H_2O = water!

When we were young, we Ladies of a Certain Age only drank water when we were thirsty. *period*! No one ever heard of keeping hydrated when we participated in sports. "They" said, "Never drink water when you exercise or you'll get stomach cramps!" Maybe our generation just didn't get thirsty or it just wasn't proper to guzzle water in public.

Nowadays all I hear from the young folks is "Gran, you've just got to stay hydrated!"

and they suggest six to eight glasses of water per day.

"Yow-zee"…If I drank that much water, I would never get out of the throne room! If I take a healthy sip now, I feel guilty for not downing the whole glass! The young folks cheer me on to, "Drink chug-a-lug." (H_2O that is)!

I have a very good bladder, but if I stayed that hydrated, my bladder would flow like the Rio Grande during spring runoff!

To add to my dilemma, here comes the transgender, trans (whatever you feel you are that day) bathrooms (actually all this topsy-turvy gender ID could work in our favor)! We have more choices when making a dash when "nature calls" after too much water!

I do think life was simpler when we were young and just girls or boys. I remember a long time ago (sixty years to be exact) I was helping a pre-school class line up for the drinking fountain and bathroom call.

A precious three-year-old boy ran up to me and asked, “Am I a boy or a girl?” Two lines were forming, and I told him with authority which line to go to! Yes, it was a simpler time when I was young!

A Happy Accident

I have always loved the sound of silence when getting away from civilization and exploring Mother Nature.

The day was glorious for my fall adventure with my two youngest grandchildren. With my two precious preschoolers in hand, we hiked up Embudito Arroyo having brought our favorite McDonald's Happy Meals.

It was our special day to experience "the sound of silence." The sun bathed us in fall warmth as a soft breeze kept us cooled. We were nurtured by the loveliness of the day as we hiked up to our gently flowing waterfall.

We arrived, having spent time chasing butterflies and avoiding cactus and buzzing bees. Nestled between the huge boulders, we arranged our blankets just so to enjoy our boxed lunches.

Before we ate, I said, "Skyler, Brik, let's be quiet and listen to the sound of silence!"

We three were very still...Unexpectedly, I loudly passed gas! So much for my lesson on the sound of silence...but I did teach them it's okay to laugh at yourself, and the kids laughed with me.

My Kaleidoscope of Joy

I found my Kaleidoscope of Joy staying part of my granddaughters' growing up experience: from precious baby days to confident young ladies in graduate school.

Samantha and J. J. make me feel cherished. They are my touch stone to the future, and we love each other unconditionally.

I cultivate making *younger* friends, but I stay loyal to my *oldies*! My old friends are just those…old friends! The zest of young friends attracts me because graduations, weddings, and baby showers keep me young at heart.

To be part of my granddaughters' lives are a real blessing for this Lady of a Certain Age! Samantha and J. J. exemplify grace and beauty and are always kind and caring. The girls have no idea how wonderful they are. Yes, I am a proud "Granny Goose!"

Becoming the Velveteen Rabbit

I have always loved the nursery story, the Velveteen Rabbit, written so eloquently by Margery Williams. When reading this sweet story to my granddaughters when they were little, it always filled my heart with love and appreciation for growing old and a little shabby around the edges.

All the years, being close to my little ones, have wrapped my heart in contentment. I am treasured and protected now they are grown up. We have fun together. Never do they make me feel like a drudge they have to check on.

Unlike the Velveteen Rabbit, I have not lost whiskers but sprouted a few that always surprise me. My girly shape has shifted, and I am a little dumpy like the Velveteen Rabbit, but I'm still me!

Brown spots and wrinkles tell my age, but it doesn't matter. I am still "Granny Goose," who has loved and been loved by Samantha and J. J. all these many years. What's happened to me in my evolution of ageing just hasn't mattered.

I can never be ugly with my loose joints and droopy eyes because my granddaughters' love has been real.

Now *I am* the Velveteen Rabbit, with years of precious baby hands and sticky kisses swirling through my immortal soul. When the little ones would cry and say, "Gran, don't ever leave us!" I would assure them I was a Guardian Angel in training and God wasn't ready for me yet! Until then, I am the Velveteen Rabbit!

Night Life

Time for bed! The ritual of a lifetime with more than a few tweaks. (Not to be confused with twerks)!

Night-lights aren't just for kids anymore! They are a necessity for this "Lady of a Certain Age!" One false step and it's a 911 call!

Easing myself into bed, works. Getting comfy with my two eccentric dogs and my two "in *charge*" cats is a production! Everybody has their set space and woebegone to the furry one that forgets his place! This is not a democracy!

Once we are strategically arranged (like packing the family car for a road trip), it's sweet dreams until the morning light. Ah, dreams! Of course we all have our style. The dogs have little barks and contented sighs, the cats purr with an occasional pussycat kiss, and I have ladylike snores. K-u-m-b-a-y-a…

BAM!

Lullaby and good night…but long before the morning light the tranquility of my sleep is shell-shocked by what I consider a schizophrenic wake-up call.

It's *BAM*! My eyelids fly open like my mind thinks it's Christmas morning! The witching hour has arrived and I'm wide awake, ready to greet the morning birdsong? Where is the gentle lightness on the horizon being the harbinger of dawn? No…horror of horrors it's 3:00 a.m., and I'm wide awake! My internal clock's ticktock has popped a spring and I'm wide awake ready to greet the morning. I'm awake and now it's time for choices! What to do?

There is the old standby, warm milk (containing tryptophan), which is an old-time remedy that sometimes works to combat sleeplessness, or then I could turn on my reading light, grab my bedtime story book, take a deep breath, relax, and read away hoping to fall asleep before greeting the morning light!

Then if I'm really "wired and fired", I could get up and clean house, which I find a dismal idea at 3:00 a.m. My next endeavor of mind meandering is to try and solve the world's problems while planning for a perfect life for my family.

I find these introspective thoughts are not the ones to produce a blissful sleep and would definitely keep me awake all night. I move my thoughts on to a patchwork of happy memories of times that glow softly in my heart. I feel warm and fuzzy doing this and I do drift off, but not immediately.

My cats are delirious with joy that I'm awake to play kitty games with them. "No way" say I to the two furry bundles of joy! It's 3:00 a.m., so they scamper off to bring me "a midnight mouse." (This is what I call unexpected gifts delivered to me after midnight)!

My dogs both sleep soundly, and I envy their power to snooze away blissfully!

Sometimes my sleepless nights are a good time to contemplate my book. The midnight dance of memory can be very self-satisfying, and all sorts of ideas hatch into reality.

I don't think there is a Lady of a Certain Age that hasn't experienced this 3:00 a.m. unwelcome wake-up call. "Sweet dreams, my ladies. May you all find your special path to lull yourselves back to sleep!"

Arise and Greet the Morning

It's outside for the pets and a mad dash to the bathroom for me. I remember the days when I just hopped out of bed.

Now it's throw the covers back, pull my knees together, roll sideways, sit up, and scoot myself swinging (I use the term loosely) my legs over the edge of the bed. Next I set my feet firmly on the floor and rise like Lazarus rising from the dead!

Next it's the dash to the bathroom, which is an Octogenarian's Olympic Event! In record time, I arrive at my destination, "the bathroom throne."

Squaring off, turning with urgency, I arrange my sleeping garments, while checking my fall line. Swish, I drop like a rock to sit just so on the "bathroom throne." Yes, gravity was involved to achieve a successful conclusion.

Standing up, all We Ladies of a Certain Age have our own personal rituals. I arise (semi-gracefully), feeling the whole procedure is a minor miracle!

One step at a time is my morning mantra! Thank you, God, for the gift of another day!

Flip, Flap, and Flutter

In my eighty-first year, a flirty hummingbird honored me. She picked the top rung of the wrought iron, lattice support of my patio to build her nest. What intrigue to watch her build from spiderwebs and lawn fluff. My lady's endeavor, which resembled a Navajo Hogan, inverted to leave the top open to nestle two raisin-sized eggs, was a wonder to behold.

Now my tiny hummingbird and I were becoming friends, so I gave her a name, Hermione. The name seemed suitable for such a whirlwind of activity and purpose.

Hermione sat on her eggs, after a fashion, as she was somewhat of a "party girl," but when the wind blew and the hail pelted, Hermione was always on duty, a real paragon of responsibility protecting her eggs soon to be hatchlings. These were remarkably perfect moments to witness.

One day I noticed two slender, black pins poking over the edge of the nest. Hermione was gone! What to do? I was afraid they were orphans...But the next day the wee bird zoomed in to feed those slender, black pin-like beaks. Hermione was a good mother and stuffed her babies with precision and patience a mystery concoction.

The following day there were little heads poking up attached to those remarkably long black pins. They waited patiently for mom to bring dinner. Now was the time to name them, Steve and Lily. Officially, I was bonded to my hummingbird family.

Hermione was a very good mother keeping Steve and Lily well fed. Never staying long at the nest she *jockeyed* in, circling the area, flying backward, zooming forward, and making a three-point landing. This miracle of motion left me awestruck!

A week later, I noticed Steve standing on Lily for his springboard to newfound flapping. One day he actually stepped wobbling, on the edge of the nest to flap, flap, flap. I thought he was going to fall, but Steve managed a fledgling two-step and stayed put. Steve was macho and kept Lily as his spring board.

Hermione swooped in for another feeding and flitted off, chirping and clicking all the way. This was a magical time for me watching out my kitchen window, the flight of my hummingbirds.

The next day, Steve was gone, but I knew the little hummingbird clicking in the tree was Steve.

Now tiny Lily was all alone in the nest, enjoying having more room being the home-alone hatchling. Preening her feathers was Lily's favorite pastime, but she became a great *flapper* too! Hermione cavorted in at regular intervals to feed her lovely daughter. Then one day Lily was gone.

I felt a holy wonderment about my hummingbird experience and an overwhelming sadness when they were gone...but were they? Now it has been three weeks and there are three hummingbirds that buzz my car when I drive home and then flip, flap, and flutter to the hummingbird feeder.

Soon they will fly off to South America... but in the spring I will watch and pray for a safe flight back to Albuquerque.

I will be so honored if they return to their Navajo nest on my back porch. The hummingbirds filled my life with light-filled moments. Always I will be humbled by the devotion of Hermione, my hummingbird, and her hatchlings, Steve and Lily.

My Yellow Brick Road

When I was a young married lady, taking time *to find yourself* was one of the fads of the day… (Frankly I didn't think I was lost, but what did I know at age twenty-six).

Having a jet pilot husband to love and cherish, three fabulous, adventurous, creative kiddos, and a variety of dogs, cats, and one hamster named Merry Chase, I didn't have time to search for me. (That was a run-on sentence for those of you who care)!

Now that I am A Lady of a Certain Age, I am sure I was never lost. (I didn't think I was at the time. I did think about it a little but didn't have the time to dwell).

As the years flew by, I had a profound realization! All along I had been traveling along "My Yellow Brick Road," which had brought me to my mature me.

What a Blessed Journey I've had. Along the way there has always been that one special friend, a soulmate.

Jack was always there for me, but there were times Jack was deployed, which made my friends all that more important! I will always treasure my good friends in my heart! Never have I felt alone! Such a great gift I was given!

I've been a lucky duck in my lifetime! No deep dark secrets or regrets haunt me. Of course, I have stumbled along the way, but there has always been an Earth Angel there to hold my hand!

Jack, my husband, is for eternity, as are my family and friends. I have had a Blessed Journey down My Yellow Brick Road, and yes, I've found myself! Really, I was never lost!

Channeling Erma Bombeck

I'm not much of a psychic, but the longer I worked on "Bedtime Stories" I felt Erma Bombeck was channeling through me. Her humor and delight at being able to laugh at herself has infused my life.

It's fun to remember how Erma made me laugh about her true antics of a young married woman and a new mother. How I identified, and to this day smile remembering Erma.

My favorite vignette Erma wrote was titled "You Are My Favorite Child." It touched my heart like nothing else I have ever read.

I love writing, and I am never alone! Erma is my spark and is inspirational through my mind's eye. As my ideas arrive on paper, I am never sure they are all mine or a touch of Erma's eternal magic flowing through me. She is my muse!

If Erma would have had a longer life, what antics of longevity would she have written about? Erma would have been the Dalai Lama of longevity!

I'm having such fun in Erma Bombeck's memory! If you haven't read Erma Bombeck's books, it's not too late to read them now. She was a brilliant, warm-hearted lady, and Oh So Special!

THE END
Or is it
THE BEGINNING?

This book would not have been possible without the help from my technical staff (My Grandchildren.)

Director

Brik Jackson Albach

Consultants

J.J. Bear Williams

Samantha Bearsmith

Skyler Brie Ann Albach

About the Author

Lloyda Albach is a fledgling 84-year-old author, who is both spry and engaging! Writing is a contact sport for her, and she has the perfect setting; the foothills of Sandia Peak on the outskirts of Albuquerque New Mexico! Lloyda enjoys the wildlife and the changing seasons in her picturesque home, which she and her husband Jack had built 45 years ago. Her views on life are both heartfelt and quirky. Lloyda looks forward to sharing her Bedtime Stories with you.

CPSIA information can be obtained
at www.ICGtesting.com
Printed in the USA
FFOW02n0508250618
47210769-49984FF